C000161538

# Clydescapes

## Inverclyde in Verse and Image

## By Iain Mills

**This book is published by Westmill Media. All profits from 'Clydescapes' will go to Ardgowan Hospice, Greenock.**

**Copyright © Iain Mills**

**First published August 2013**

**Printed by Largs Printing Company (LPC)**

## Introduction

Inverclyde is a very special place. This area of coast and hill, town and village on Scotland's west coast is dominated by its great river and marked by the drive of its people. The stunning landscapes and gritty character have been beautifully captured by film director Ken Loach. I asked Ken – who directed the film *Sweet Sixteen* in Inverclyde – to sum up what Inverclyde means to him. He came up with the following:

*'We learned to respect the people of Greenock and the surrounding area during the time we spent working there. The landscape is extraordinary – dramatic with its steep hillsides and its river but also domestic, with its rows of terrace houses. But it is the people who make it special. Hard times give people strength but also many difficulties. The struggle to surmount those has been very tough. Sometimes that struggle can end in failure. But it also produces acts of generosity and heroism that count far more than the good deeds of those who live in softer conditions'*

To sum Inverclyde up as beautifully and eloquently as Ken Loach has is indeed a challenge, but this is what I've aimed to do in this book. For over a year now I've been putting together this collection of verse and images, most ably assisted by local photographers. The 36 poems, the accompanying three-line haikus and 41 images are the result of this. We hope it does justice to the area.

One of the themes that run through the book is change: that Inverclyde does not remain the same for long; that its economy has undergone major changes as have its landscapes and environment. The book also celebrates Inverclyde's heritage and its people: with each change, people have to adjust, and this can often be a painful process. People ghost

3

through the poems, some well-known and some anonymous: Sammy, who lost his older brother at Gallipoli, James Watt, Birdie Bowers, Robert Thom, Mary Campbell and others. In poems such as 'William Street' it's my own ancestors that cast ghostly shadows on the cobbles (and with three grandparents born in Inverclyde there are a lot of shadows!). However, Inverclyde has taken change on board while retaining the characteristics that mark it out as unique within Scotland.

Reaction to the poems and photographs has been very positive. The actor Richard Wilson – who was brought up in Inverclyde – commented as follows on reading the book: *'Looking through the pages has brought back many memories of Clydeside. I'm sure it will be read by many who know that part of the world.'*

I believe that a collection like this is a first for Inverclyde. It is my hope that the poems enhance the readers' appreciation of the images and that the images enhance the poems. It has given me great pleasure to produce this book and I'm delighted that such a worthy cause as Ardgowan Hospice will benefit from its success.

Iain Mills, August 2013

## Acknowledgements

Many people should be thanked for their support in the making of this book. In particular I would like to thank local photographers from the Inverclyde and Greenock Camera Clubs for the stunning images that they've produced. Gaie Brown and Campbell Skinner from these clubs also applied their organisational skills superbly to help pull these contributions together. Without their efforts there would have been no book. I'm also grateful to Texas Instruments, who were the book's main sponsors. Tommy Thomson, Mr Craig of Windy Hill, Lucinda Shaw Stewart and others allowed their names, homes or families to be mentioned in the poems. Inverclyde Council's support for and promotion of the book is most welcome. The assistance of Clydeport, and the Greenock Telegraph with marketing is very much appreciated. Last and not least I must thank my wife, Jackie, for all the cups of coffee, cheesecake and encouragement that kept the creative wheels turning and for her valued input to the editing of the collection.

## List of Poems

**List of Images**

| 31 | 79 | Sugar Shed | Gaie Brown |
|----|----|----|----|
| 32 | 81 | Bouverie Street | Campbell Skinner |
| 33 | 83 | Newark Castle (1) | Gaie Brown |
| 34 | 85 | Timber Ponds, Parklea | Gaie Brown |
| 35 | 87 | Windy Hill, Kilmacolm | Mr Craig |
| 36 | 88 | Memorial, Well Park | Gaie Brown |
| 37 | 91 | Container Terminal, dusk | Gaie Brown |
| 38 | 92 | Newark Castle (2) | Gaie Brown |
| 39 | 93 | Greenock Cut (2) | Gaie Brown |
| 40 | 94 | Wemyss Bay Station (2) | Roy Dunlop |
| 41 | 95 | Cloch Point | Bill Clark |

## Clydescapes

This great river

Has many facets, each a fresh-cut diamond,

Each, taken with the others, adding to the whole:

Clutha spread like shimmering Chinese silk

Or churning, white-frothed, hurling its anger at the shore,

Branded indelibly in folk memory, respected

By each successive generation for what it's given

But also for what it's taken, this Jekyll and Hyde:

Men lost, ships gone - never to return,

And trade of empire, the sea-borne prosperity

That floated shipyard and sugar,

Shaping our towns, etching our identity.


This is our inheritance, the unrelenting tides,

The beaded, pebble-laced shore,

Sandbank and bay;

We kneel in the lapping wash as great ships pass,

Our Clydescapes turn, the familiar rearranged,

Reflected in the light on ever-changing waters.


Our Shenandoah
Old Man River, Father Thames
Its flow our lifeblood

## At the Custom House

On November nights
The mists that wisp around the fluted columns
Carry distant echoes:
Boots scarting on causeys
And trudging up the gangplanks
Of emigrant ships; voices
Ringing out, speaking
Of Winnipeg or New Brunswick.

A damp autumn leaf
Drifts to the ground like
A tear-stained handkerchief;
Voices fade into darkness.

Water laps below the walkway;
A seagull, quizzical on a lamp post
Seeks its own departed brood
On the west wind,
And only grooves scored in the cobbles
Mark the slow scrape of time.

At the Custom House
Autumn falls as morning mist
On time-etched cobbles

## **Wemyss Bay Station**

The first train out of Wemyss Bay,
Glasgow Fair Monday:
A thin straggle of commuters
Heads for the city,
Unseeing, blinkered by routine.

The 9.50 from Glasgow pulls in
Sardined with holidaymakers,
The tin skin of the carriages
Barely containing the
Excitement; the anticipation.

As one the crowd
Surges across the concourse,
Streams towards the pier,
A symphony of laughter, banter;
The percussive clatter of buckets and spades.

First timers look up in wonder at
The intricate interlace of
Beams and girders; the scent
Of verdant hanging baskets;
Cheering at their first glimpse of the steamer.

As the boat sails west
Porpoises arc to starboard and
Railmen get their station back,
The only sound a stiff brush sweeping
The debris of childhood dreams.

Rothesay-bound children
Scream with anticipation
As the train pulls in

## Barranca

Looking out from a bar
In Barranca,
Gazing past the lovers' pergola
Where soaring black vultures
Rise and fall on the updraughts
Above the brittle cliffs,
The pale grey curtain of the sky
Their backdrop.
Beneath them,
The churn of the Pacific
Rakes at the black sand shore,
Threatening the land.

To the north a watery sun
Struggles over Miraflores
But fails to illuminate.

On another day,
By Cloch Point,
A coal black submarine
Cleaves south through a slate sea;
Seagulls scavenging in its wake
Scrape the gaunt, grey sky,

Their whiteness jarring, out of place,

Like snowflakes falling on charcoal.


No watery sun,

No lovers' trysts,

Nor chill Pacific mists:

Just this black shape

Carving through the grey of sea and sky;

A different vulture.


Heading for Coulport
Nuclear submarine cleaving
The slate-grey river

## **Old Customs….**

Tommy Thomson used to tell me
About the angels' share:
'That golden, whisky aroma' he said,
'Would knock you on your back',
And a smile would light his face.

'Men detoured by the customs sheds
On their way to their work
Just to get a whiff of it'
And he was there again,
Eyes closed, breathing it in.

And then he'd frown:
'What got to me' he'd say,
'Was all those angels up there
Getting drunk on it
While us mere mortals
Down here were gasping for a drink.'
And just to make his point
He'd inhale deeply,
Savouring the memory.

Two parts oxygen
One part whisky, breathe it in
And savour slowly

## Sammy

Each year at the war memorial
They huddled to hear your bugle,
Watching your cold-tipped fingers
Squeeze notes from reluctant brass,
Breathing life into the past.

Some said your notes were bullets,
Fired off in undiminished rage
For a dead brother:
Salvoes sprayed over bowed heads
Lest they forget.

Some said your notes were doves,
Kissing the air above the crowd,
Soaring over rooftops,
Settling softly on shoulders
Lest we forget.

You never said:
Closing your eyes you
Coaxed the Last Post from pursed lips,
Walked slowly past the wreaths
And off through the crowd.

In Gallipoli
Stained earth in the olive groves
Tells of Gourock men

## The Mariner's Preparations

Everything stowed,
Weeks of provisioning over:
All set to sail at dawn.

As the sun dips low o'er the dock breast
We gather on the Mid Quay
Talking of journeys past.

The imagined scent
Of the Indies is almost tangible;
We inhale in expectation.

Seagulls scream around
Victoria Tower; children's laughter
Tinkles in the soft evening.

All is buffed,
Hopes and brass gleaming,
Timber polished till it shines.

Harbour lights
Guard the perimeter,
Quietly eking out reflections.

Anticipation

Cracks like dry lightning

Amidst still rigging.

All set to sail at dawn

Leaving Greenock in our wake

Once more.

The quiet waters
Lap around our restless ship
The Atlantic waits

## View from the Hill

Ribbons of streetlight
Hold Gourock in a soft, sodium glow,
Quietness hugs the land,
Pierced only by the odd shrapnel
Of stray shouts, a car horn;
A train threads its way eastwards
Like a stretched, twisting glow-worm.

A slow wave of darkness
Deepens across the stepped hillsides
Above the curving bay;
Soft reflections streak the water
Swirling in a ferry's wake;
Parks and woods are deep pools,
Their features secret, hidden.

On main roads street lamps fend off
The night, removing its rough edges;
Even the ancient standing stone,
Silent above the old town
Never sees the real shadows,
No longer feels the deep impenetrable night
Of darker times.

Seen from the Lyle Hill
Gourock spreads beneath its lights
In soft, orange glow

27

# The Inverkip Coach

Pink blossom from gnarled cherry trees

Drifts over a high sandstone wall

And swirls along the roadside;

Worshippers from the auld kirk

Descending the lang, steep brae

Turn up their collars against

The snell, north-westerly,

Pausing at the corner where their ways part,

Their farewells accompanied

By the percussive jangle

Of the Shaw Stewarts' carriage.


To the west, o'er the arched brig,

The Inverkip Inn stands, solid and

Square, the haunt of travellers and

Drouthy locals not always seen

In the pews on Sundays:

A farm labourer leans in its doorway

Hearing the deep insistent drumming

Of a stagecoach in the west,

And wonders at folk able to

Travel in such style

On the long and winding road to Greenock.

> The Inverkip Inn
> Aye gave weary travellers
> Welcome bed and board

## Lunderston

It's the kind of sunset
Along this quiet shore
When every silhouetted rock is a seal
Every swaying seaweed frond a fish.

The staccato clatter of crabs' claws on stone
Taps over the shushing surf
While a sea of petrol hues
Barely moves,
And time is measured in a sky
Of darkening blue.

The old red sandstone
Four hundred million years old
Has been here before

## Land

This hard land, this rocky place,

Basalt and sandstone strong under my heels,

A place of rain and moss and the curlew's cry,

Where generations walked and talked

And cried and died

Against a backdrop of trees and walls and hearths:

These are the substance beneath my feet.


On a hillside a farmer's curses

Spur on the sheepdog;

It twists and turns the flock around, backlit in the low sun,

Penning them, bringing in the strays:

I stand on Dunrod rounding up the generations,

Bringing them into focus,

Clothing them and the land they live in.

This land is full, this land is empty,

The voices muted, the voices ringing out;

Colours muted in the sepia wash,

And the same birds sing for a thousand years,

And the same dogs howl at the autumn moon.


Flying home

Gazing down from thirty thousand feet,

*Clydescapes*

On specks of fields and flattened hills,

Blue-dotted lochs in miniature,

This small patch of world seems the same

As any other;

Insignificant against ice or coral,

More nondescript than peak or forest:

But from this crag, with the wind slipping through

The tussock grass and

The laverocks keening overhead,

And the reality of rock and stream and ruin

Spread out below,

The timelessness floods over me, banishing

The blurred borders between the living and the dead,

Rendering the pace of deeper change

Infinitesimal.

Time doesn't pass here
It accumulates; our past
Sits with our present

## 'Birdie', 29th March 2012

On a cold-bright March morning
We gathered near the place
Of Henry Bowers' birth,
The sharp wind spearing the esplanade
A breeze by Antarctic standards;
Our shivers more from association
Than measurable cold.

We counted the hundred years
Since his final days, we
Measured his life with words like
Courageous, heroic and brave;
Schoolchildren strewed cream roses
On opaque waters.

On that hushed and sunlit morning
We opened the tent flap, peering in,
Smelling the gangrene, the rotting flesh,
Sensing the battle between faith and despair
As those weak and frozen men
Stared into the sunless abyss.

Death in a blizzard
Reflections in Greenock on
Scott's expedition

LIEUTENANT H.R. "BIRDIE" BOWERS, R.I.N.
BORN HERE 1883
Died with Captain R.F. Scott and his party
on the return journey from South Pole, 1912

## Waterfront

Walking the Esplanade,
River spread to the north,
A minke whale, seeking Greenland
Arches and rises,
Its flanks pleated, rippling,
Crowds of watchers applaud
And unseen icebergs dot the firth.

Tall ships in a heat-haze,
Piper shrill in the crow's nest as
Sailors scramble in bleached rigging;
People throng the waterfront,
Spirits higher than the Glenlee's masts
As other, fainter, ghost ships
Lift anchor and slip away.

By the waterfront
Tides turn like the times.

Steel grey river drifts
Past hazy morning figures
Going with the flow

## 1930: The Emigrant's Song

The coulter cuttin deep an straight
Thru Manitoba's cauld, dark clay,
Ow'r by the lonely steadin's lea,
The snaws o' winter lie in May.

Bleak an threatenin, heavy clouds
Roll on in frae distant seas,
Scrapin ower the great flat fields
Sae heavy bellied on the breeze

Ah mind o' leavin Princes Pier,
Ma brither's face amangst the throng,
As tears o sorrow sting ma een,
The partin cruel, the journey lang.

This nicht we'll tak the darkenin loan
Tae the dim licht o' MacPherson's barn
Tae hear Gillespie's auld, sad tunes
Return us tae oor distant land.

Whaur the sun sinks gowden ower the Clyde
Warmin the whin-clad hills o hame,
A land no rich like these dark fields,
A land Ah'll never see again.

> Canadian cauld
> Seeps intae ma agein' banes
> Ah wish Ah wis hame

## The Auld Kirk Yard, Inverkip Street

A willow arches over the gate

Like a curtain in time:

Beyond its green drapes

The dead stand

As sandstone and granite slabs,

John Galt recumbent, Robert Mill erect,

The surface of the stones

Exfoliating history.


The letters rot and crumble

Like willow leaves in autumn;

November's low sun

Throws lengthening shadows

Across the turf:

The stones, like sundials, mark

Passing time

And the slow creep of decay.


Frost on John Galt's grave
The Annals of the Parish
In rimy letters

## Where the tides run

At Cloch Point
The tides can run and turn
With little warning;
The lighthouse signs the danger
In black and white.

Along this brooding shore,
The tides of war
Have ebbed and flowed,
Surging and eddying
But rarely still.

Great grey convoys
Slipped stealthily in and out;
Cunarders, full of grace and hope
Were captured in time as ghosts
In the sweep of the lighthouse beam.

When the tranquil sea
Darkens to churning maelstrom
We search for the light

## Soundscape, Cornalees

Closing my eyes at dusk,

Sieving the sounds that wash around me;

The aching cry of the curlew,

The laverock's evening chatter,

Set against the drone of an aircraft

Weaving through wispy southern clouds.


The sough of the wind

Caresses the reed beds;

Threshing wings beat water

As geese skim the surface,

Straining for elevation

Ahead of Dunrod Hill.


Along the dimming loch-shore

Wavelets paw the stony bank

And a stirring trout sends ripples

Murmuring towards me;

Over by Gryffe a fox's bark

Challenges the stillness of the evening.


Evening, Loch Thom
Simmering twilight soundscape
Ripples around me

## James Watt  (Kent his Faither)

Jimmy Watt
Aye steamin
Bent ower kettles
Big face beamin

'Gang oot son'
Widnae listen
Heid designin
Some new piston

Crackin enjins
'n brilliant pumps
Boy fae Greenock
Came up trumps

Unit a power
Took his name
But doon oor way
He's jist wee James

He thinks he's sumdy
Hero in his ain midden
Ah kent his faither!

## Cross of Lorraine

Memories in concrete

Seven decades on:

The anchor casts

Its maritime shadows;

The cross honours

Our loss, their loss,

In once calm waters.


Beyond the cross

The white-flecked river

And the mottled hills of Cowal

Form the backdrop as we

Remember once more

The cruel, relentless undertow

Of harrowing times.


The beauty of the
Scene in this high place can change
With your perspective

## Tale of the Bank

A riveting place,

Its memories cut from sheets of steel

Still oxy-acetylene sharp;

Communities welded by sweat and metal

And fused by fire.

Inverclyde in a bunnet:

Working boots on rainy cobbles

Steel hulls gliding to the Clyde,

Fattening towns stretching and climbing,

Gasping above the shrouding fog.

Silicon replaces steel:

Weeds sprout round desolate docks

Cushioning the toppling cranes,

Ghost yards exorcised for business parks and

Bunnets just for golf and on we go.

But where will it lead now, this tale?

A greener Inverclyde

Growing leaner and fitter,

All dressed up with someplace to go

A place whose ship has finally come in?

> Steel leviathan
> Cleaves the dawn's grey waters as
> Memory's chains rattle

## Heilan Mary

She's driftin in an oot o sleep,
Beside the bed, her brither weeps,
He watches death's relentless creep
    Upon her broo:
Pale fingers touch her burnin cheek
     It's ower late noo.


Her fevered mind won't gie her rest,
She sees a ship, a voyage west,
The passion burnin in her breast
     Oh, such is bliss!
An savours wi her final breath
     His last fond kiss.


        Her life afore her
        Or so it seemed, the Indies
        Wi her bonnie Rab

## Gourock Pier

Smell of sea salt,
Squealing gulls,
See-sawing gangplanks and
The shoof of fishing lines
Cast in hope.

Oil rainbows water,
Tides pour from trains,
Tarry ropes lurk like coiled snakes
As the Jeanie Deans sweeps in
With heaving decks.

Blast of the horn,
Ropes snare bollards,
Gang planks manhandled, then
Sandals, shoes and eager boots
Scuff and stomp.

Jellyfish,
Fading accordion strains,
Paddle-wheels churning as
Seabirds swoop in their wake
Out to the west.

Fading sounds and smel's
Doon the watter remembered
On sun-lit mornings

## Amongst the Stones

Into this landscape,

January:

Above the estuary the high moors

Are washed with a hard light;

The low sun

Highlights each

Ridge and furrow;

Painted hillside gives up

The gash of prehistoric track

Whilst around me

The stones write patterns

Among the sedges,

Circles, squares and lines,

Archaeology etched

Timelessly:

My shadow lengthens as

My own significance diminishes.


Ancient tumbled stones
Worn smooth and lichen-covered
Signposting the past

## The Sailors' Kirk

They climbed thick brown rope

To reach the loft

Within the Old West Kirk,

And gazed through stained glass windows

At passing, multi-coloured

Topsails and tall masts;

Calloused fingers traced over carvings,

Knowing the three covered cups

To be the gentry's mark.

Their faith could move mountains,

But what did it take

To shift a whole church?

Willing hands, steely determination,

A sailor's deep sense of

What could not be lost:

Stone, slate and time-marked timber

Dismantled and numbered;

Rebuilt by skilled and caring hands.

To the east,

Harland and Wolff's yard

Sank like the Titanic…

An old church moved west
To make space for a shipyard:
Only the church remains

## Rain

Fine rain drifts quietly over
Battery Park's grassy sprawl,
Softening the edges of the landscape,
Dulling the noises gnawing at its fringes,
Draping the hills in grey shrouds.

Many a parade's been rained on here
Banners of all hues dampened in the drizzle:
Rechabites, Orangemen, Socialists,
Rallying in their cheering thousands,
Their soggy footprints long since gone.

Maybe the beauty of the rain lies in
The way it wipes the slate clean,
Rinsing out the cultural landscape:
When the sun bursts through
A fresh start gleams through the clearing mists.

In Battery Park
Echoes of distant parades
And waving banners

## Tram Lines

Rusting iron set in cobbles:

Tram lines, as a way of thinking,

Left little room to manoeuvre;

Trundle on them from west to east,

Rattle along from east to west,

Never deviating from the straight and narrow.

Progress was made, no doubt;

Electric replaced horse-drawn,

Women joined the crews,

But always this was travel

With nowhere left to go

Except off the rails.

July fifteenth, '29,

The last tram, a number 10

Left Cathcart Square

For Ashton terminus;

No detour of the imagination waiting

To take it past the scrap-heap.

In West Blackhall Street

A sense of loss still lingers.

The 'Sparkies' followed
The shoogly one-way journey
To transport's graveyard

## **Well Park**

Is this the Grian Chnoc?

Levelled now, sanitised,

A hill once standing in the sun

Yet casting shadows

Of its own.

Plunge to the depths of its well,

Sift through pagan silt,

Sieve the detritus of past lives

And find

Not rays of sunshine

But struggle and loss fingerprinted in

The thick oozing mud:

Fragments of a pot, a

Broken, corroded brooch,

Deer bones and dog skull.

At ground level,

Scour the bushes

For signs of where we are now:

A broken wine bottle,

Rusting cans, a plastic bag,

The disenfranchised
Slumped on benches, wrapped in oblivion.

The past has not disappeared;
The present merely gives a new stage
To older shadows
Still flickering over
Grian Chnoc.

Shadows linger on
The sunny hill where Greenock
Grew into the light

## William Street

We've walked this street
A century and a half,
Leaving our invisible DNA trail
On the granite setts,
Marking our territory
In quiet and unassuming ways:

One put up those railings,
One trekked daily to the dock breast
To fit out ships,
A son designed the vessels
That carried the great diaspora,
Keeping the genetic lines afloat.

We've walked by James Watt's house and school
Past the fluted columns
Of the Mid Kirk,
Up the steep brae, clutching at those railings
And past the bank that died,
Shared landmarks in a shared lineage.

*Clydescapes*

What does it mean, this continuity?

Does it add up to anything at all?

A pre-determined route

In some faint map of time

Or nothing but coincidence?

And who will follow?

Quiet, timeless flow
Through Greenock's streets; people with
A common history

## The Cut

Sun slants through reeds
Warming sluggish waters,
Pondweed thrives in this murky soup,
A heron on stick leg
Eyes the shadows.

Rain slashes Dunrod Glen,
Rivulets force-feed the channel,
Water surges down its course,
Past rotting wood and iron sluice,
Stirring up much more than silt.

White cascades, long gone, churning,
Driving the Merino Mill,
The giant wheel dipping, spinning,
Weaving the fabric
Of people's lives.

After the rains,
Dragonflies skim translucent pools
And all is still.

Genius channelled in
Power-bringing waters - or just
Some Thom-foolery?

## Demolition

A lonely figure picks his way
Through fields of debris
On carpets of glass;
Refraction throws rainbows
From a thousand slivers
To penetrate a hundred shadows.

He sees a hole where the hearth was
A hole where the heart was, where
Cobwebs veil torn wallpaper.

The detritus of his bulldozed dreams
Trips him up and
Almost brings him down;
Lifting an empty bottle
He smashes it against
Long-forgotten fears.

A photo lies in the dimming light
Faded to monochrome, splintering as
He grinds it under heel.

Low winter sun

Stretches the shadows

Of broken lamp-posts;

He scrapes his feet on

A fallen stone, fearful

Of taking the mud with him.


Collar up, hands thrust in pockets,

He turns his back

On a bitter, nagging wind.


Can you dismantle
Walls and memories this way
And leave no traces?

## The Sugarhouse

Our heritage is framed
With iron girders
And built up brick by brick.
Names scaffold its structure,
Antigua and Tobago Street;
Westburn and Lyle.
Grand west-end mansions,
Built with sugar,
Sweetened many lives.

Inside the brooding, empty sheds
An odour of the Indies
Permeates the brickwork:
Jamaica's legacy is still stacked high
In the mind's eye;
The sounds of stevedores play
On a timeless loop.
But peer in darkened corners,
And catch a fleeting glimpse
Of slavery's deeper shadows

At the Sugarhouse
The past is written
In bricks and mortar.

The Old Sugarhouse
Iron and brick monument
To another age

## **The Bouverie**

Crossing the sea with

A wife, a child and some weaving skills;

Modest dreams – a roof above,

Food on the table, some warmth in the winter chill,

And to see a son grow and survive

Unlike his brother in the Tyrone clay,

To go from day to day…


It rises like

Some monolithic cliff

Above the Port, its bulk

A refuge to the man from the flatlands;

Simple aspirations more than met

By its sandstone heights,

And teeming closes.


A job in the mill to pay the rent

And a room at the day's end

In the Bouverie.


> On Bouverie Street
> Sheer stone ramparts towering
> Above the old port

## Crane and Turret

As the land yields anew,

Time ticks slowly on the Newark shore,

The years measured in the ripening of the apples,

The clack of the looms, glass breaking on hulls;

Buildings rise and tumble, waves

Of people, rich and poor,

Wash across the land and ebb away.


Now the crane and turret

Stand side by side,

Unlikely neighbours;

Steel and stone throw long shadows

On the water, brief minutes

In the years of other tides

Come and gone.



Everything changes,
Nothing stays the same for long
Upon Newark shore

## Timber Ponds, Parklea

Stand here
As cold dawn splashes the eastern sky
And hear the wading birds greet
Its colours with their din;
The oyster catcher's screech thrown at the light
Like shards of broken glass,
The thin cry of the curlew following
Its solitary arc.

Waders sift the oozing mud
As wavelets suss against the shore;
The timbers rise, sea-gnawed stumps,
Ochre and algae-green against the light
Like rotted teeth;
Overhead two terns trace velvet patterns,
Through air dripping with their songs,
The distant, growing growl of traffic
The drone to their grace notes.

Seasoning timber
Floats in the salty water
As time and tide stop

## Windy Hill

Horizontals and verticals, warp and weft,
The fabric of existence;
The horizontals - ordinary lives,
The verticals the aspirations.

Colours work in combination,
The heather and the morning rose,
Lit by a Port-Vendres sun,
Light and shade, shade and light.

One-ness of stone and glass,
Textile and engraving
Purity of line allied with
Integrity of form.

Design blends
Function and ornamentation,
We revel in the black and white,
The yin and yang.

At snowy Windy Hill
We gaze in silence, trying
To catch the essence in
The detail and the broad-brush.

Macintosh vision,
His design realised in
Wood, stone and mortar

## Women of Inverclyde

Strong women

Forged with keels of steel;

Through temperance days

The rivets that held it all together,

Helping their men, their weans to

Steer clear of the

Reefs and shallows.


Iron clad women,

Resilient, determined,

Making a little go a long way,

Working miracles till the next pay day,

Calming stormy waters and

Standing proud in troubled times,

Laying it on the line.


In this new landscape

Of derelict slipways, empty yards,

Are they still out there,

The red amongst the grey?

> Whit's fur dinner Da?
> Better go an ask yer Maw
> Fur Ah've nae money

# BONUS IMAGES

The photographs on the next five pages were too good to leave out

## About the author

Iain Mills, when not writing, built a career in education, and is well known in Inverclyde as a teacher, university lecturer and education adviser.

He writes in Scots and English for both adults and young people, and his published works include poems, short stories, a play and several academic articles. These have appeared in anthologies such as New Writing Scotland and A Braw Brew.